Managing Editor
Ina Massler Levin, M.A.

Editor
Eric Migliaccio

Contributing Editor
Sarah Smith

Creative Director
Karen J. Goldfluss, M.S. Ed.

Cover Design
Tony Carrillo / Marilyn Goldberg

Teacher Created Resources, Inc.
6421 Industry Way
Westminster, CA 92683
www.teachercreated.com

ISBN: 978-1-4206-5975-7

©2007 Teacher Created Resources, Inc.
Reprinted, 2011 (PO4776)

Made in U.S.A.

This book belongs to

_____

Ready·Set·Learn

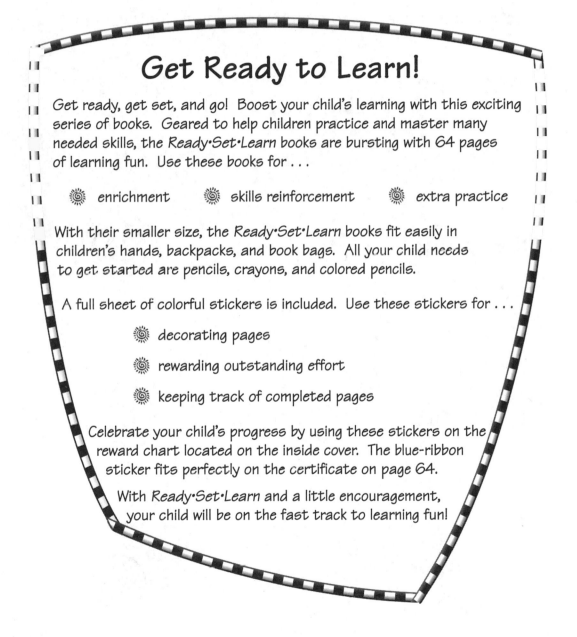

Get Ready to Learn!

Get ready, get set, and go! Boost your child's learning with this exciting series of books. Geared to help children practice and master many needed skills, the *Ready·Set·Learn* books are bursting with 64 pages of learning fun. Use these books for . . .

☀ enrichment   ☀ skills reinforcement   ☀ extra practice

With their smaller size, the *Ready·Set·Learn* books fit easily in children's hands, backpacks, and book bags. All your child needs to get started are pencils, crayons, and colored pencils.

A full sheet of colorful stickers is included. Use these stickers for . . .

☀ decorating pages

☀ rewarding outstanding effort

☀ keeping track of completed pages

Celebrate your child's progress by using these stickers on the reward chart located on the inside cover. The blue-ribbon sticker fits perfectly on the certificate on page 64.

With *Ready·Set·Learn* and a little encouragement, your child will be on the fast track to learning fun!

Coins

Directions: Draw a line to match the coins to their values.

one cent

five cents

ten cents

twenty-five
cents

4

Identifying Pennies

Directions: Color the coins that are pennies with a brown crayon. Put an **X** on each coin that is not a penny.

Identifying Nickels

Directions: Color the coins that are nickels with a blue crayon. Put an **X** on each coin that is not a nickel.

6

Identifying Dimes

Directions: Color the coins that are dimes with a green crayon.
Put an **X** on each coin that is not a dime.

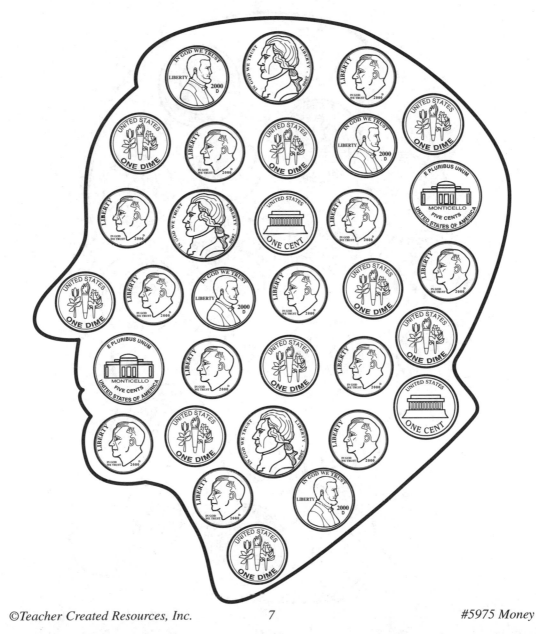

Identifying Quarters

Directions: Color the coins that are quarters with a red crayon. Put an **X** on each coin that is not a quarter.

Identifying Coins

Directions: Color the pennies with a red crayon. Color the nickels with a yellow crayon. Color the dimes with a green crayon. Color the quarters with a blue crayon.

= Red   = Green

= Yellow   = Blue

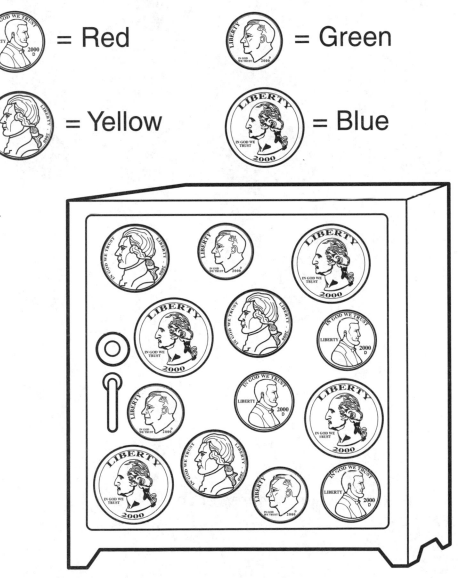

Which One?

Directions: Circle the right answer.

1. Which one is a quarter?

   (A)   (B)    (C)    (D)

2. Which one is a penny?

   (A)   (B)   (C)   (D)

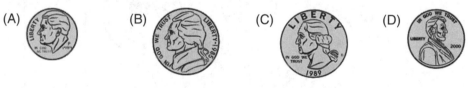

3. Which one is a nickel?

   (A)   (B)   (C)   (D)

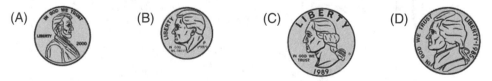

4. Which one is a dime?

   (A)   (B)   (C)   (D)

5. Name the coin. Write your answer on the line.

 _____

How Many?

Directions: Answer the questions.

1. How many are quarters?

_____

2. How many are pennies?

_____

3. How many are dimes?

_____

Matching Sets

Directions: Look at the first box of pennies, nickels, dimes, and quarters on the *left*. Find a box of pennies, nickels, dimes, and quarters on the *right* that contains the same amount. Draw a line to match the sets. Repeat with the other boxes of coins.

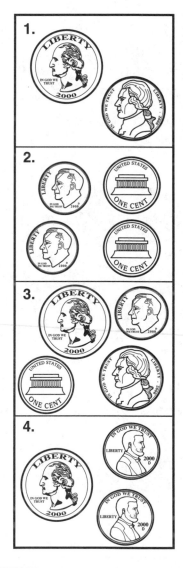

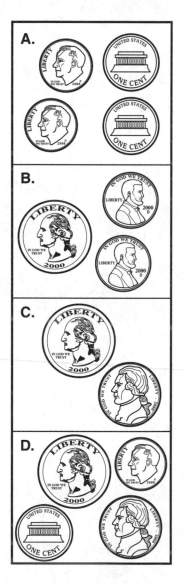

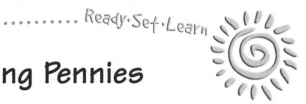

Counting Pennies

Directions: Look at the number at the beginning of each row of pennies. Color that number of pennies.

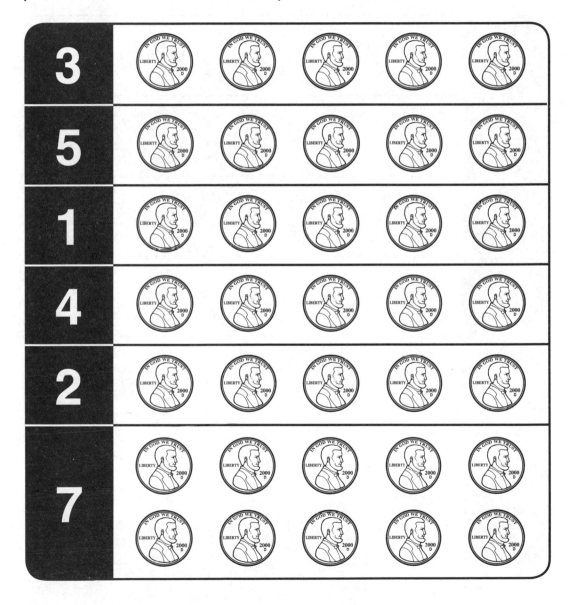

Counting Nickels

Directions: Look at the number at the beginning of each row of nickels. Color that number of nickels.

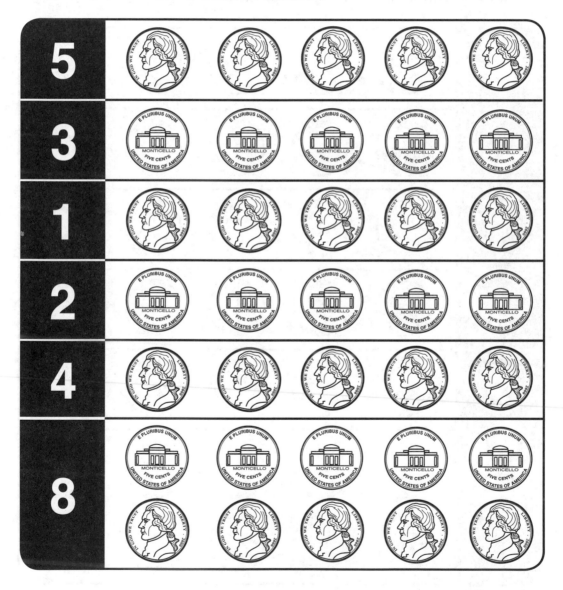

Counting Dimes

Directions: Look at the number at the beginning of each row of dimes. Color that number of dimes.

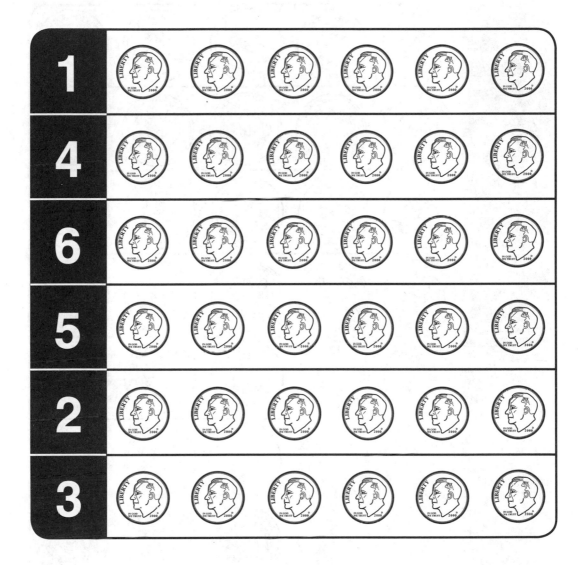

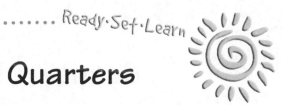

Counting Quarters

Directions: Look at the number at the beginning of each row of quarters. Color that number of quarters.

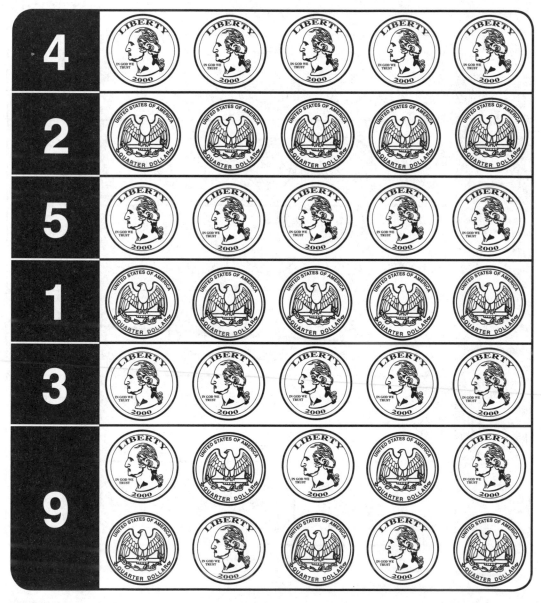

16

©Teacher Created Resources, Inc.

Working with Pennies

Directions: Color in the pennies to show how much each item costs.

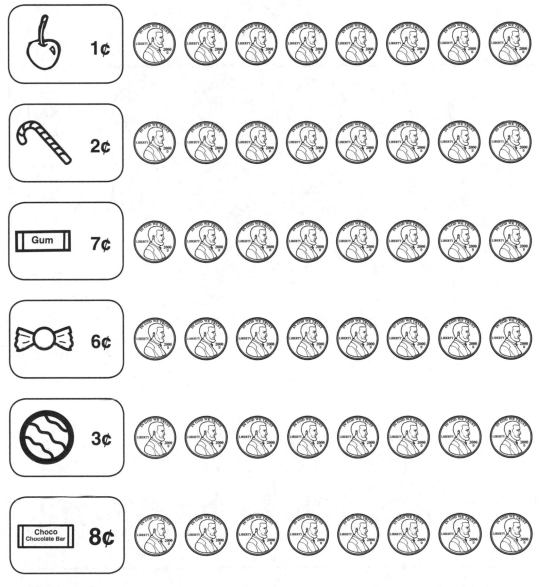

Buying with Pennies

Directions: Look at the price tag on each item. Color the number of pennies needed to buy the item.

A penny is worth one cent.   **1 penny = 1¢**

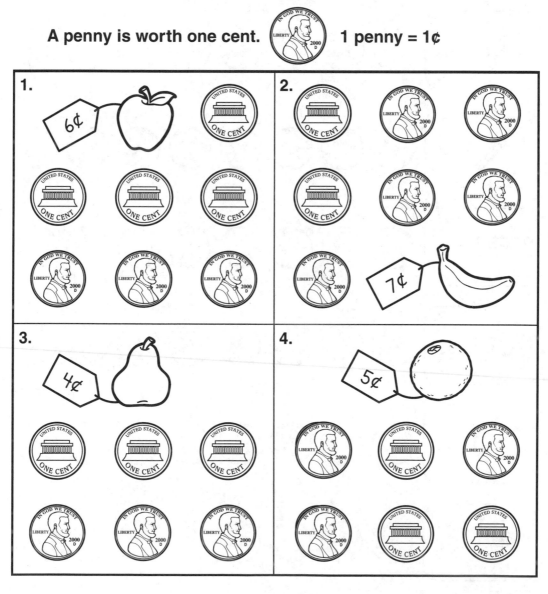

Buying with Nickels

Directions: Look at the price tag on each item. Color the number of nickels needed to buy the item.

A nickel is worth five cents.

5   10   15   20   25

1. 15¢

2. 25¢

3. 30¢

4. 20¢

Buying with Dimes

Directions: Look at the price tag on each item. Color the number of dimes needed to buy the item.

A dime is worth 10 cents.

10   20   30   40   50

20

Buying with Quarters

Directions: Look at the price tag on each item. Color the number of quarters needed to buy the item.

25	**50**	**75**	**100**

A quarter is worth 25 cents.
Every four quarters = one dollar = $1.00

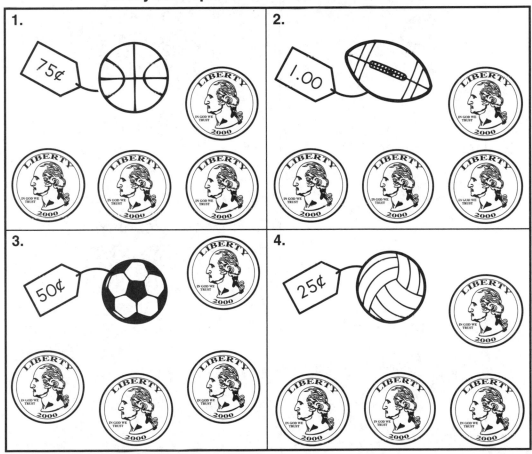

Money Matters

Directions: Read and answer each question.

1. How many cents?

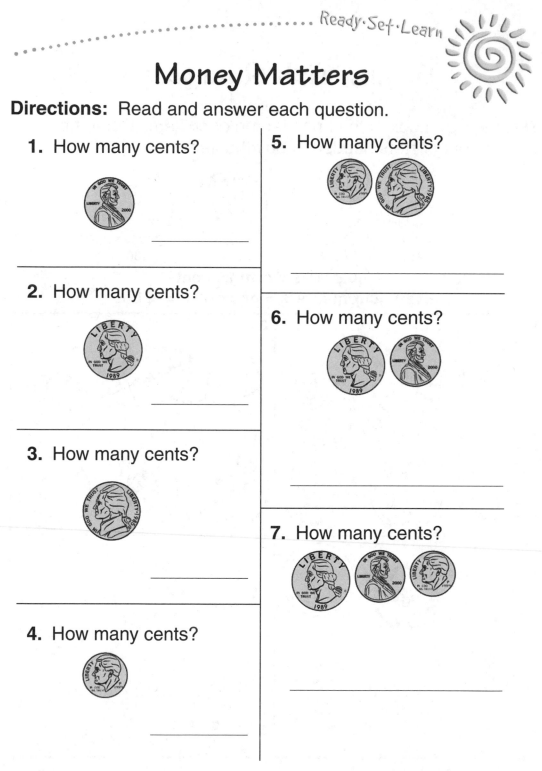

_____

2. How many cents?

_____

3. How many cents?

_____

4. How many cents?

5. How many cents?

_____

6. How many cents?

_____

7. How many cents?

_____

Sets of Coins

Directions: Read each question. Circle the correct answer.

1. Which set shows 5¢?

(A)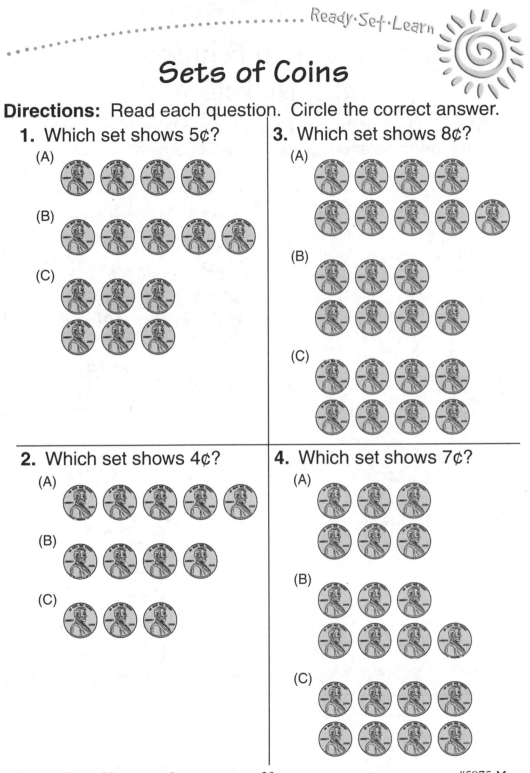

(B)

(C)

3. Which set shows 8¢?

(A)

(B)

(C)

2. Which set shows 4¢?

(A)

(B)

(C)

4. Which set shows 7¢?

(A)

(B)

(C)

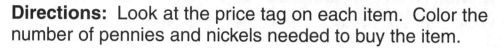

Buying with Pennies and Nickels

Directions: Look at the price tag on each item. Color the number of pennies and nickels needed to buy the item.

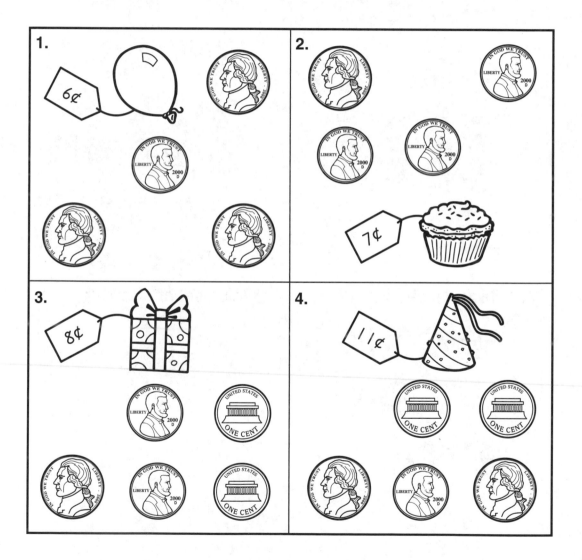

Buying with Pennies, Nickels, and Dimes

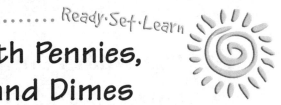

Directions: Look at the price tag on each item. Color the number of pennies, nickels, and dimes needed to buy the item.

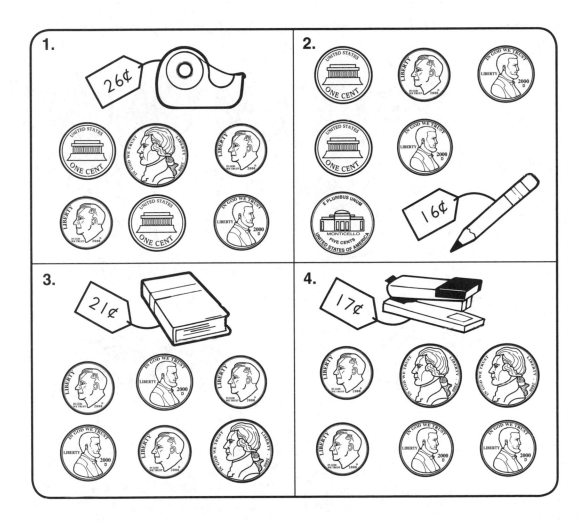

1. 26¢

2. 16¢

3. 21¢

4. 17¢

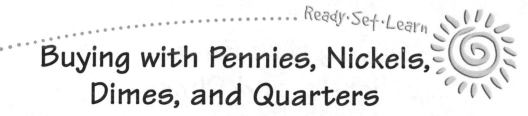

Buying with Pennies, Nickels, Dimes, and Quarters

Directions: Look at the price tag on each item. Color the number of pennies, nickels, dimes, and quarters needed to buy the item.

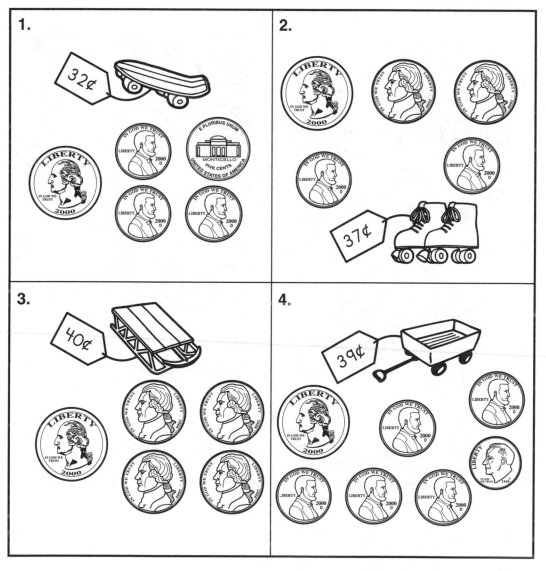

Counting Money

Directions: Count the amount of money in each row. Write the total.

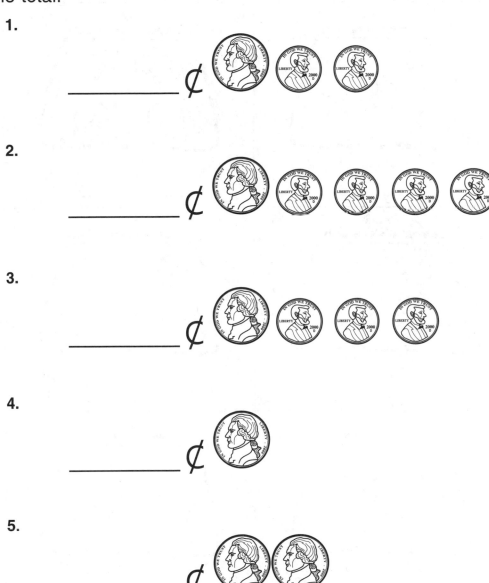

1.

_____ ¢

2.

_____ ¢

3.

_____ ¢

4.

_____ ¢

5.

_____ ¢

Coin Purses

Directions: Count the coins in the coin purses. Write the total amount of money on the lines.

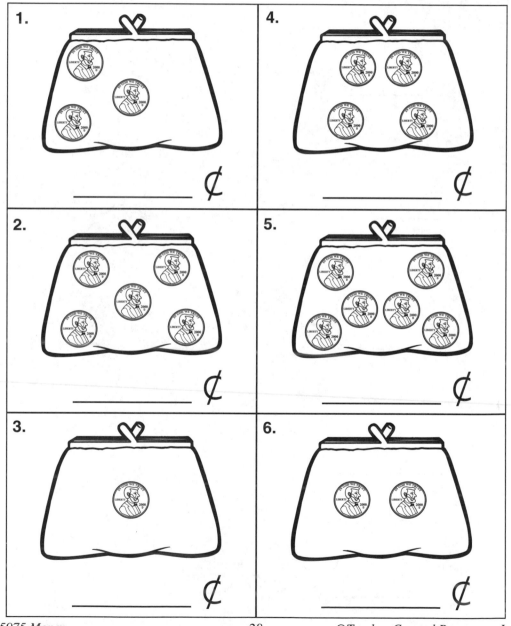

1. _____ ¢

2. _____ ¢

3. _____ ¢

4. _____ ¢

5. _____ ¢

6. _____ ¢

More Coin Purses

Directions: Count the coins in each coin purse. Write the total amount of money on the line.

1.

_____ ¢

2.

_____ ¢

3.

_____ ¢

4.

_____ ¢

5.

_____ ¢

6.

_____ ¢

Count Your Money

1. How much money do you have?

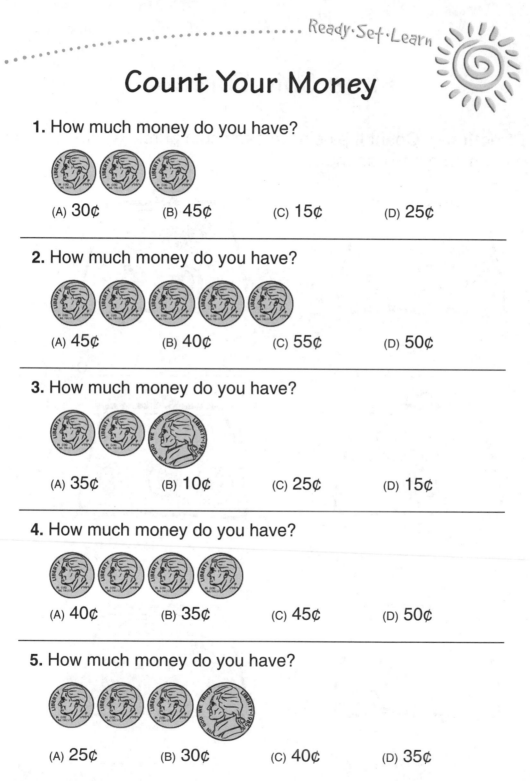

(A) 30¢   (B) 45¢   (C) 15¢   (D) 25¢

2. How much money do you have?

(A) 45¢   (B) 40¢   (C) 55¢   (D) 50¢

3. How much money do you have?

(A) 35¢   (B) 10¢   (C) 25¢   (D) 15¢

4. How much money do you have?

(A) 40¢   (B) 35¢   (C) 45¢   (D) 50¢

5. How much money do you have?

(A) 25¢   (B) 30¢   (C) 40¢   (D) 35¢

Count Your Coins

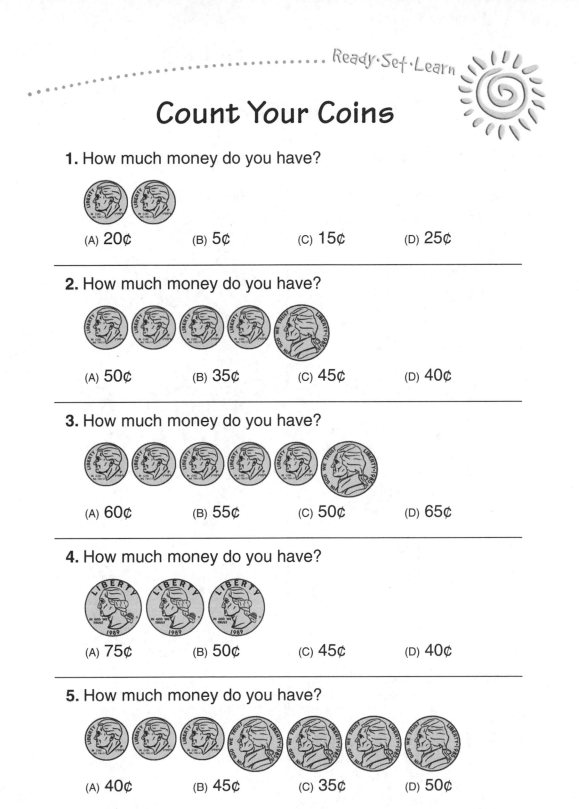

1. How much money do you have?

(A) 20¢   (B) 5¢   (C) 15¢   (D) 25¢

2. How much money do you have?

(A) 50¢   (B) 35¢   (C) 45¢   (D) 40¢

3. How much money do you have?

(A) 60¢   (B) 55¢   (C) 50¢   (D) 65¢

4. How much money do you have?

(A) 75¢   (B) 50¢   (C) 45¢   (D) 40¢

5. How much money do you have?

(A) 40¢   (B) 45¢   (C) 35¢   (D) 50¢

Sets of Cents

Directions: Read each question. Circle the answer.

1. Which set shows 50¢?

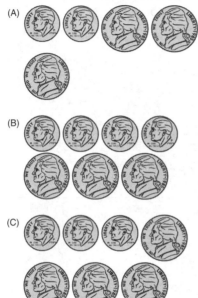

(A)

(B)

(C)

2. Which set shows 25¢?

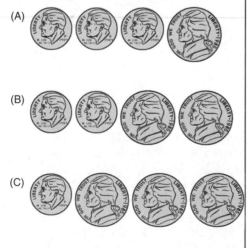

(A)

(B)

(C)

3. Which set shows 70¢?

(A)

(B)

(C)

         32   *©Teacher Created Resources, Inc.*

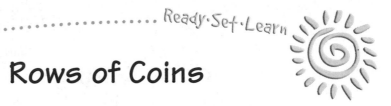

Rows of Coins

Directions: Read and answer each question.

1. How much money do you have? _____

2. How much money do you have? _____

3. How much money do you have? _____

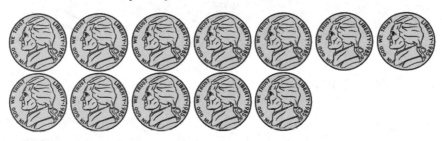

4. How much money do you have? _____

5. How much money do you have? _____

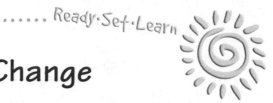

Loose Change

Directions: Read and answer each question.

1. How much money is this? _____

2. How much money is this? _____

3. How much money is this? _____

4. How much money is this? _____

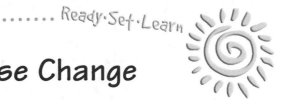

More Loose Change

Directions: Read and answer each question.

1. How much money do you have? _____

2. How much money do you have? _____

3. How much money do you have? _____

4. How much money do you have? _____

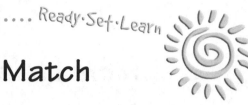

Price Tag Match

Directions: Color the coins needed to match each price tag.

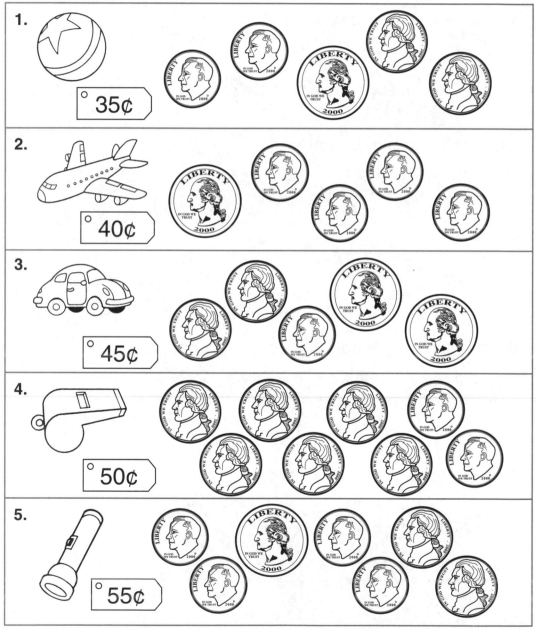

1. 35¢

2. 40¢

3. 45¢

4. 50¢

5. 55¢

Dollars and Cents

Directions: Draw a line from each row of coins to the correct amount.

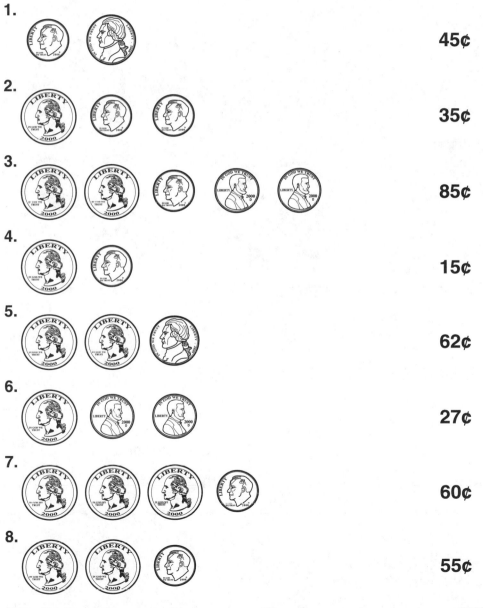

1.   45¢

2.   35¢

3.   85¢

4.   15¢

5.   62¢

6.   27¢

7.   60¢

8.   55¢

Toy Show

Directions: Count the coins. Answer the questions.

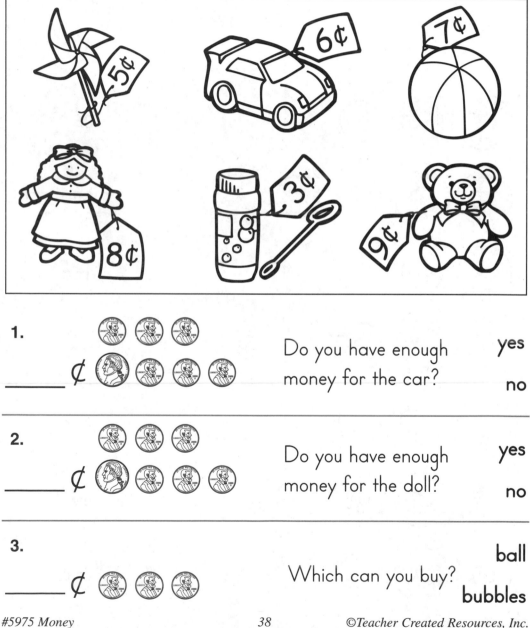

1. _____ ¢   Do you have enough money for the car?   yes   no

2. _____ ¢   Do you have enough money for the doll?   yes   no

3. _____ ¢   Which can you buy?   ball   bubbles

Grocery Shopping

Directions: What does it cost? Write the total amount for each basket.

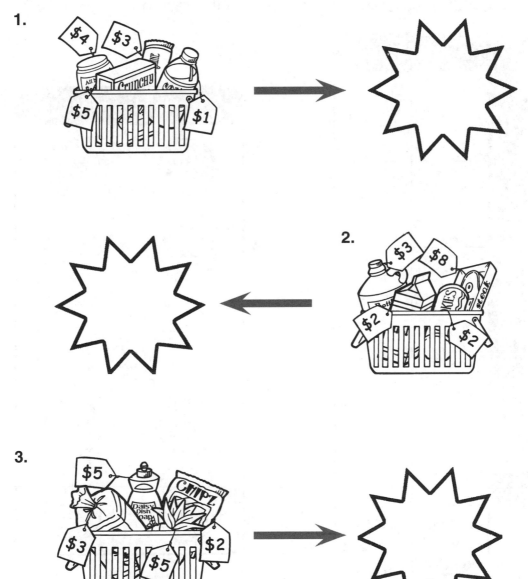

Graphing Pennies

Directions: Count the pennies that show heads. Color that number of squares on the graph. Count the pennies that show tails. Color that number of squares on the graph.

Heads or Tails		
5		
4		
3		
2		
1		

Heads or Tails

Graphing Dimes

Directions: Count the dimes that show heads. Color that number of squares on the graph. Count the dimes that show tails. Color that number of squares on the graph.

Heads or Tails		
5		
4		
3		
2		
1		

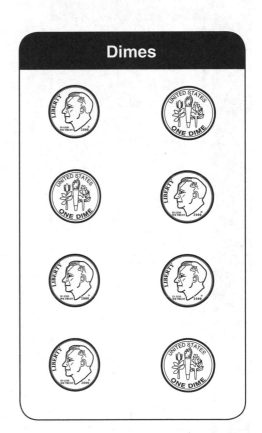

Dimes

Graphing Quarters

Directions: Count the quarters that show heads. Color that number of squares on the graph. Count the quarters that show tails. Color that number of squares on the graph.

Heads or Tails		
5		
4		
3		
2		
1		

Quarters

Graphing Coins

Directions:
Count the pennies. Color that number of squares on the graph.
Count the nickels. Color that number of squares on the graph.
Count the dimes. Color that number of squares on the graph.
Count the quarters. Color that number of squares on the graph.

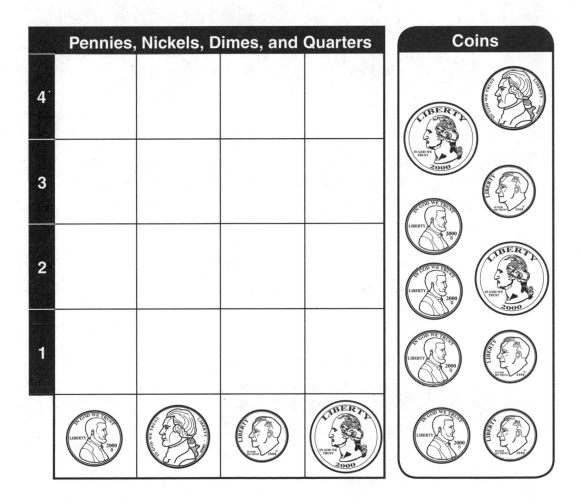

Money Addition

Directions: Read each question. Circle the answer.

1. Add the amounts. Use the coins to help.

$$45¢ + 1¢ = \underline{\hspace{2cm}}¢$$

(A) 46¢   (B) 48¢   (C) 43¢   (D) 44¢

2. Add the amounts. Use the coins to help.

$$31¢ + 22¢ = \underline{\hspace{2cm}}¢$$

(A) 28¢   (B) 33¢   (C) 29¢   (D) 53¢

3. Add the amounts. Use the coins to help.

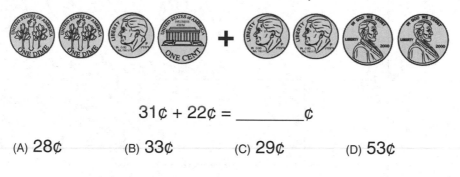

$$21¢ + 6¢ = \underline{\hspace{2cm}}¢$$

(A) 27¢   (B) 26¢   (C) 14¢   (D) 15¢

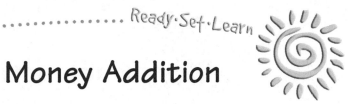

More Money Addition

Directions: Read each question. Circle the answer.

1. Add the amounts. Use the coins to help.

$$41¢ + 2¢ = \underline{\hspace{2cm}} ¢$$

(A) 37¢   (B) 38¢   (C) 43¢   (D) 46¢

2. Add the amounts. Use the coins to help.

$$27¢ + 11¢ = \underline{\hspace{2cm}} ¢$$

(A) 38¢   (B) 15¢   (C) 28¢   (D) 16¢

3. Add the amounts. Use the coins to help.

$$11¢ + 15¢ = \underline{\hspace{2cm}} ¢$$

(A) 17¢   (B) 7¢   (C) 6¢   (D) 26¢

Money Subtraction

Directions: Read and answer each question.

1. Subtract the amounts. Use the coins to help.

$$35¢ - 3¢ = \underline{\hspace{1.5cm}}¢$$

2. Subtract the amounts. Use the coins to help.

$$22¢ - 2¢ = \underline{\hspace{1.5cm}}¢$$

3. Subtract the amounts. Use the coins to help.

$$30¢ - 2¢ = \underline{\hspace{1.5cm}}¢$$

More Money Subtraction

Directions: Read and answer each question.

1. Subtract the amounts. Use the coins to help.

31¢ − 21¢ = _____¢

2. Subtract the amounts. Use the coins to help.

12¢ − 3¢ = _____¢

3. Subtract the amounts. Use the coins to help.

26¢ − 6¢ = _____¢

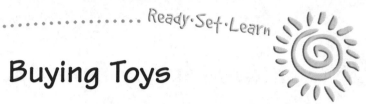

Buying Toys

Directions: Pretend that you were sent to the toy store to buy some toys. Use the pictures to find the answers to the questions.

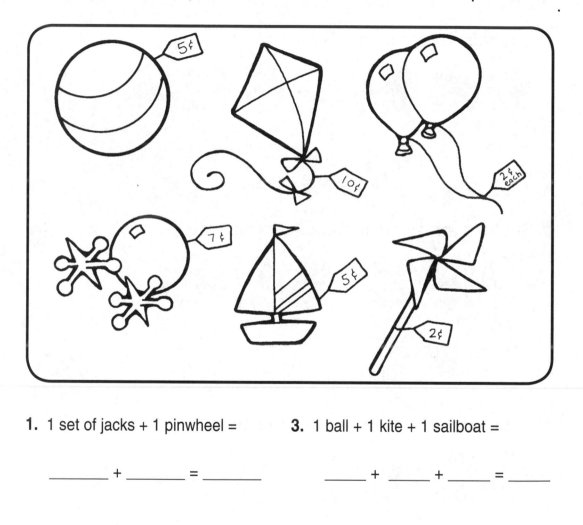

1. 1 set of jacks + 1 pinwheel =

    _____ + _____ = _____

2. 1 balloon + 1 ball =

    _____ + _____ = _____

3. 1 ball + 1 kite + 1 sailboat =

    _____ + _____ + _____ = _____

4. 1 kite + 1 set of jacks + 1 boat =

    _____ + _____ + _____ = _____

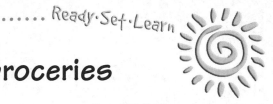

Buying Groceries

Directions: Use the prices in the box below to figure out the price of these groceries. One has been done for you.

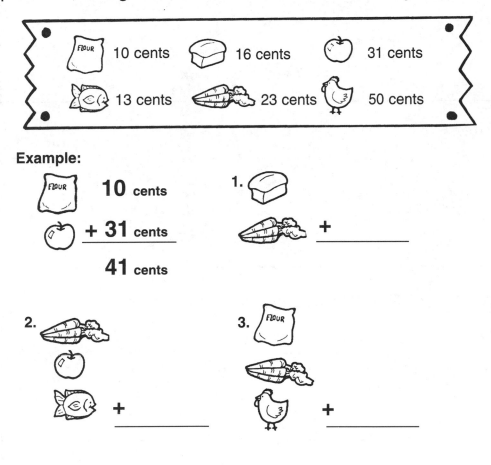

FLOUR 10 cents   16 cents   31 cents

13 cents   23 cents   50 cents

Example:

FLOUR **10** cents

+ 31 cents

41 cents

1.   + _____

2.   + _____

3.   + _____

Challenge: How much would . . .

☆ 3 chickens cost? _____

☆ 5 sacks of flour cost? _____

Comparing Prices

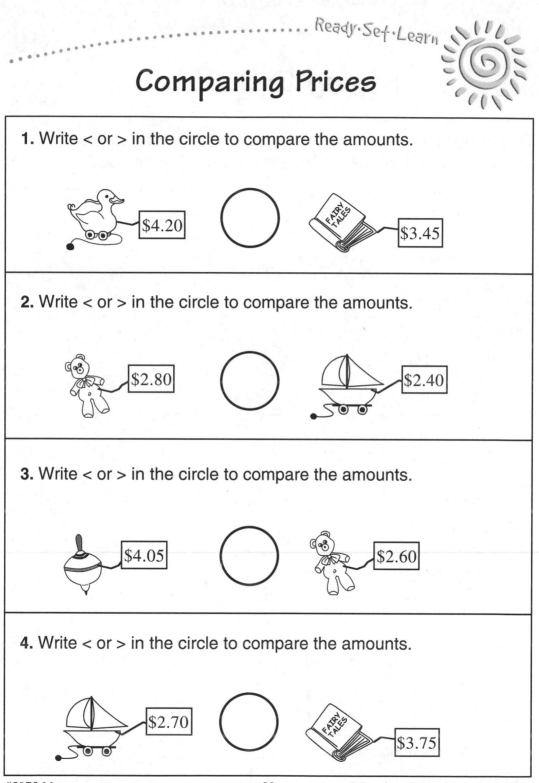

1. Write < or > in the circle to compare the amounts.

$4.20   ◯ $3.45

2. Write < or > in the circle to compare the amounts.

$2.80   ◯ $2.40

3. Write < or > in the circle to compare the amounts.

$4.05   ◯ $2.60

4. Write < or > in the circle to compare the amounts.

$2.70   ◯ $3.75

Ring Me Up!

Directions: Use the prices in the bins to help you add up your grocery bill for each of the shopping carts below.

Oranges	Bananas	Pies
53¢	20¢	29¢

Carrots	Apples
20¢	15¢

1.

2.

3.

4.

Coin Charts

Directions: Use the charts to answer the questions.

1. The chart shows the total number of coins. What amount is shown on the chart? Circle your answer.

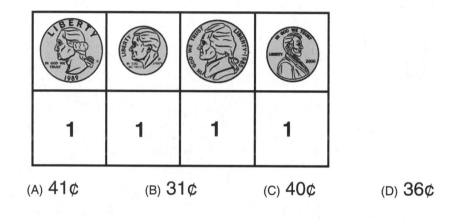

(A) 41¢   (B) 31¢   (C) 40¢   (D) 36¢

2. The chart shows the total number of coins. What amount is shown on the chart? Circle your answer.

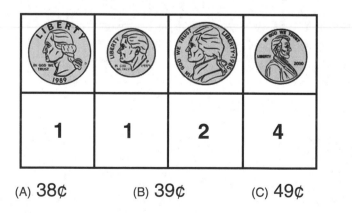

(A) 38¢   (B) 39¢   (C) 49¢   (D) 44¢

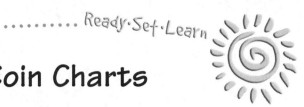

More Coin Charts

Directions: Use the charts to answer the questions.

1. The chart shows the total number of coins. What amount is shown on the chart? Circle your answer.

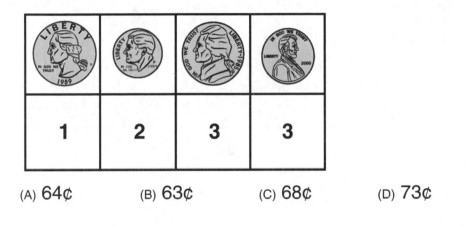

(A) 64¢   (B) 63¢   (C) 68¢   (D) 73¢

---

2. The chart shows the total number of coins. What amount is shown on the chart? Circle your answer.

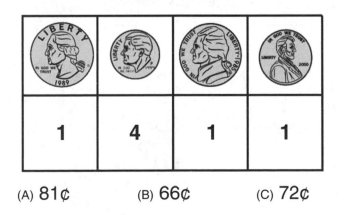

(A) 81¢   (B) 66¢   (C) 72¢   (D) 71¢

Add Up the Cost

1.

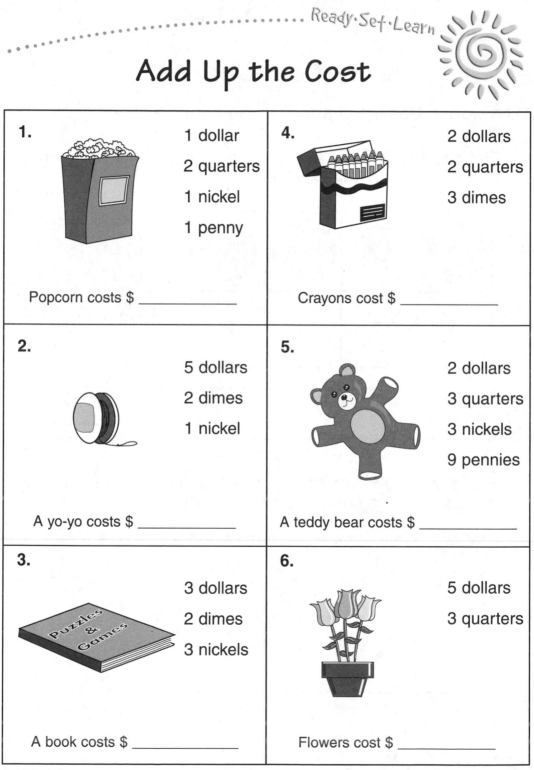

1 dollar

2 quarters

1 nickel

1 penny

Popcorn costs $ _____

4.

2 dollars

2 quarters

3 dimes

Crayons cost $ _____

2.

5 dollars

2 dimes

1 nickel

A yo-yo costs $ _____

5.

2 dollars

3 quarters

3 nickels

9 pennies

A teddy bear costs $ _____

3.

Puzzles & Games

3 dollars

2 dimes

3 nickels

A book costs $ _____

6.

5 dollars

3 quarters

Flowers cost $ _____

54

Chunk of Change

Directions: Look at the amount of money each item costs. Subtract the total from the amount of coins you have to find out how much change you will get back. Put your answer in the box at the end. The first one has been done for you.

Object You Buy	Amount You Pay	Change You Get Back
1. 47¢		3¢
2. 39¢		
3. 19¢		

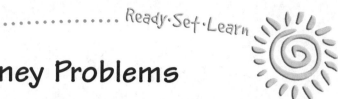

Money Problems

Directions: Read each question. Circle the correct answer.

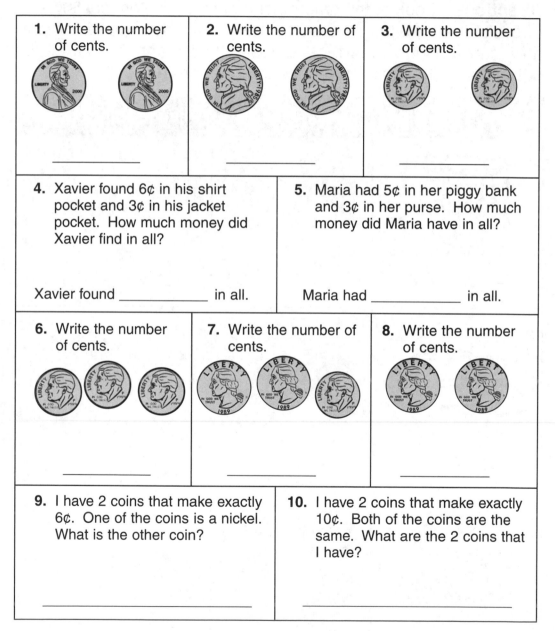

1. Write the number of cents.	**2.** Write the number of cents.	**3.** Write the number of cents.
_____	_____	_____

4. Xavier found 6¢ in his shirt pocket and 3¢ in his jacket pocket. How much money did Xavier find in all?

Xavier found _____ in all.

5. Maria had 5¢ in her piggy bank and 3¢ in her purse. How much money did Maria have in all?

Maria had _____ in all.

6. Write the number of cents.	**7.** Write the number of cents.	**8.** Write the number of cents.
_____	_____	_____

9. I have 2 coins that make exactly 6¢. One of the coins is a nickel. What is the other coin?

_____

10. I have 2 coins that make exactly 10¢. Both of the coins are the same. What are the 2 coins that I have?

_____

More Money Problems

Directions: Read each question. Circle the correct answer.

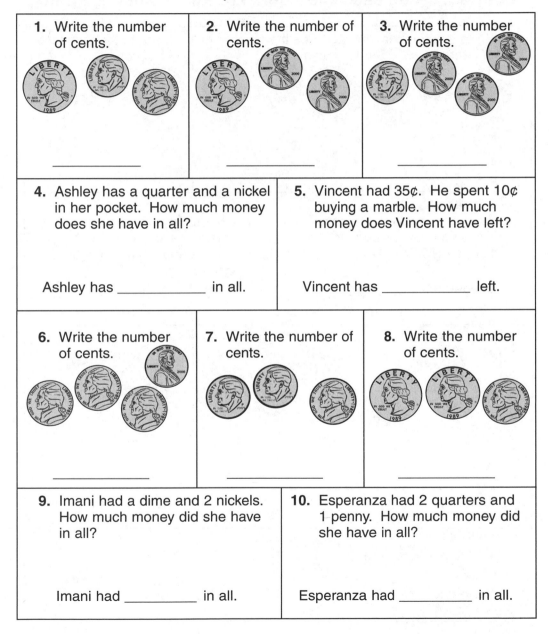

1. Write the number of cents.

_____

2. Write the number of cents.

_____

3. Write the number of cents.

_____

4. Ashley has a quarter and a nickel in her pocket. How much money does she have in all?

Ashley has _____ in all.

5. Vincent had 35¢. He spent 10¢ buying a marble. How much money does Vincent have left?

Vincent has _____ left.

6. Write the number of cents.

_____

7. Write the number of cents.

_____

8. Write the number of cents.

_____

9. Imani had a dime and 2 nickels. How much money did she have in all?

Imani had _____ in all.

10. Esperanza had 2 quarters and 1 penny. How much money did she have in all?

Esperanza had _____ in all.

Money Matters

Directions: Read each question. Circle the correct answer.

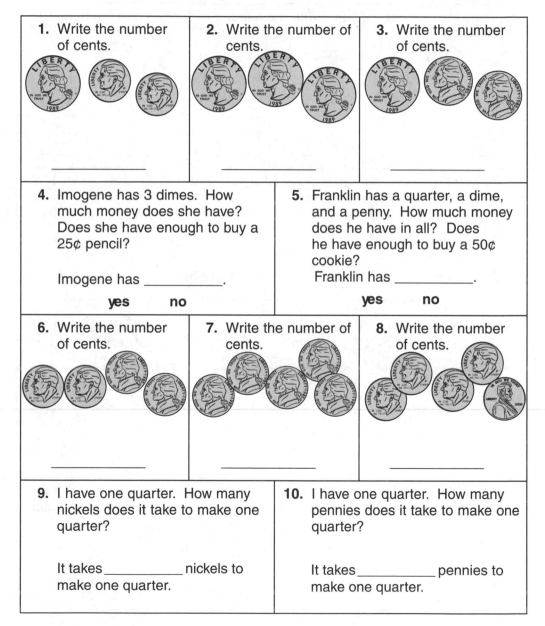

1. Write the number of cents.

_____

2. Write the number of cents.

_____

3. Write the number of cents.

_____

4. Imogene has 3 dimes. How much money does she have? Does she have enough to buy a 25¢ pencil?

Imogene has _____.

yes   no

5. Franklin has a quarter, a dime, and a penny. How much money does he have in all? Does he have enough to buy a 50¢ cookie?

Franklin has _____.

yes   no

6. Write the number of cents.

_____

7. Write the number of cents.

_____

8. Write the number of cents.

_____

9. I have one quarter. How many nickels does it take to make one quarter?

It takes _____ nickels to make one quarter.

10. I have one quarter. How many pennies does it take to make one quarter?

It takes _____ pennies to make one quarter.

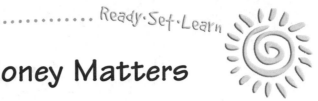

More Money Matters

Directions: Read each question. Circle the correct answer.

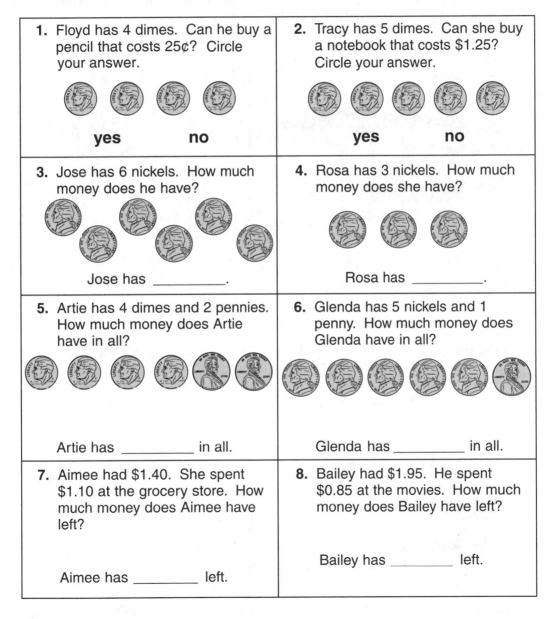

1. Floyd has 4 dimes. Can he buy a pencil that costs 25¢? Circle your answer.

yes   **no**

2. Tracy has 5 dimes. Can she buy a notebook that costs $1.25? Circle your answer.

yes   **no**

3. Jose has 6 nickels. How much money does he have?

Jose has _____.

4. Rosa has 3 nickels. How much money does she have?

Rosa has _____.

5. Artie has 4 dimes and 2 pennies. How much money does Artie have in all?

Artie has _____ in all.

6. Glenda has 5 nickels and 1 penny. How much money does Glenda have in all?

Glenda has _____ in all.

7. Aimee had $1.40. She spent $1.10 at the grocery store. How much money does Aimee have left?

Aimee has _____ left.

8. Bailey had $1.95. He spent $0.85 at the movies. How much money does Bailey have left?

Bailey has _____ left.

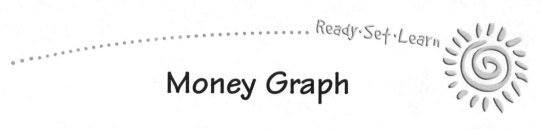

Money Graph

1. The table shows how many of each coin Mike has in his bank. How much money does Mike have?

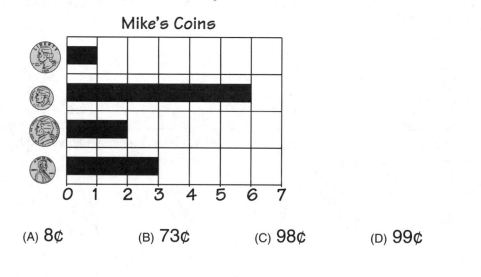

Mike's Coins

(A) 8¢   (B) 73¢   (C) 98¢   (D) 99¢

---

2. The table shows how many of each coin Stephanie has in her bank. How much money does Stephanie have?

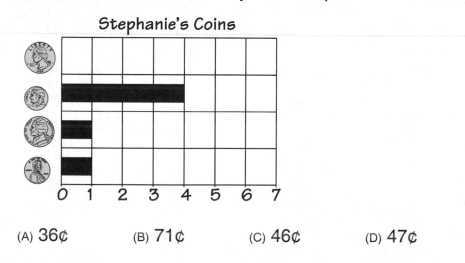

Stephanie's Coins

(A) 36¢   (B) 71¢   (C) 46¢   (D) 47¢

Answer Key

Page 10
1. C 3. B 5. penny
2. B 4. B

Page 11
1. 4 2. 7 3. 6

Page 12
1. C 2. A 3. D 4. B

Page 17
1. Color 1 penny. 4. Color 6 pennies.
2. Color 2 pennies. 5. Color 3 pennies.
3. Color 7 pennies. 6. Color 8 pennies.

Page 18
1. Color 6 pennies. 3. Color 4 pennies.
2. Color 7 pennies. 4. Color 5 pennies.

Page 19
1. Color 3 nickels. 3. Color 6 nickels.
2. Color 5 nickels. 4. Color 4 nickels.

Page 20
1. Color 3 dimes. 3. Color 5 dimes.
2. Color 2 dimes. 4. Color 4 dimes.

Page 21
1. Color 3 quarters. 3. Color 2 quarters.
2. Color 4 quarters. 4. Color 1 quarter.

Page 22
1. 1 4. 10 7. 36
2. 25 5. 15
3. 5 6. 26

Page 23
1. B 2. B 3. C 4. B

Page 24
1. Color 1 nickel and 1 penny.
2. Color 1 nickel and 2 pennies.
3. Color 1 nickel and 3 pennies.
4. Color 2 nickels and 1 penny.

Page 25
1. Color 2 dimes, 1 nickel, and 1 penny.
2. Color 1 dime, 1 nickel, and 1 penny.
3. Color 2 dimes and 1 penny.
4. Color 1 dime, 1 nickel, and 2 pennies.

Page 26
1. Color 1 quarter, 1 nickel, and 2 pennies.
2. Color 1 quarter, 2 nickels, and 2 pennies.
3. Color 1 quarter and 3 nickels.
4. Color 1 quarter, 1 dime, and 4 pennies.

Page 27
1. 7 3. 8 5. 10
2. 9 4. 5

Page 28
1. 3 3. 1 5. 6
2. 5 4. 4 6. 2

Page 29
1. 7 3. 30 5. 27
2. 11 4. 35 6. 54

Page 30
1. A 3. C 5. D
2. D 4. A

Page 31
1. A 3. B 5. D
2. C 4. A

Page 32
1. C 2. C 3. A

Page 33
1. 80¢ 3. 60¢ 5. 40¢
2. 65¢ 4. 50¢

Page 34
1. 29¢ 3. 42¢
2. 29¢ 4. 16¢

Page 35
1. $1.50 3. 24¢
2. $1.04 4. 99¢

Page 36
1. Color 1 quarter, and 1 dime (or 2 nickels).
2. Color 4 dimes.
3. Color 1 quarter, 1 dime, and 2 nickels.
4. Color 2 dimes and 6 nickels.
5. Color 1 quarter, and 3 dimes
   (or 2 dimes and 2 nickels).

Answer Key (cont.)

Page 37
1. 15¢ 3. 62¢ 5. 55¢ 7. 85¢
2. 45¢ 4. 35¢ 6. 27¢ 8. 60¢

Page 38
1. 11¢, yes 2. 11¢, yes 3. 3¢, bubbles

Page 39
1. $13 2. $15 3. $15

Page 40
heads = 5, tails = 4

Page 41
heads = 5, tails = 3

Page 42
heads = 5, tails = 4

Page 43
pennies = 4, nickels = 1, dimes = 3, quarters = 2

Page 44
1. A 2. D 3. A

Page 45
1. C 2. A 3. D

Page 46
1. 32 2. 20 3. 28

Page 47
1. 10 2. 9 3. 20

Page 48
1. 7¢ + 2¢ = 9¢ 3. 5¢ + 10¢ + 5¢ = 20¢
2. 2¢ + 5¢ = 7¢ 4. 10¢ + 7¢ + 5¢ = 22¢

Page 49
1. 16 + 23 = 39 cents
2. 23 + 31 + 13 = 67 cents
3. 10 + 23 + 50 = 83 cents
   Challenge: 3 chickens cost $1.50;
   5 sacks of flour cost 50¢.

Page 50
1. > 3. >
2. > 4. <

Page 51
1. 53¢ + 20¢ = 73¢
2. 20¢ + 29¢ + 15¢ = 64¢
3. 20¢ + 20¢ + 20¢ + 20¢ + 29¢ = $1.09
4. 20¢ + 20¢ + 20¢ + 15¢ + 15¢ + 53¢
   = $1.43

Page 52
1. A 2. C

Page 53
1. B 2. D

Page 54
1. $1.56 3. $3.35 5. $2.99
2. $5.25 4. $2.80 6. $5.75

Page 55
1. 50¢ – 47¢ = 3¢ 3. 20¢ – 19¢ = 1¢
2. 45¢ – 39¢ = 6¢

Page 56
1. 2¢ 4. 9¢ 7. 60¢ 10. nickels
2. 10¢ 5. 8¢ 8. 50¢
3. 20¢ 6. 30¢ 9. penny

Page 57
1. 40¢ 3. 13¢ 5. 25¢ 7. 25¢ 9. 20¢
2. 27¢ 4. 30¢ 6. 16¢ 8. 55¢ 10. 51¢

Page 58
1. 45¢ 4. 30¢, yes 7. 25¢ 10. 25
2. 75¢ 5. 36¢, no 8. 41¢
3. 35¢ 6. 30¢ 9. 5

Page 59
1. yes 5. 42¢
2. no 6. 26¢
3. 30¢ 7. 30¢
4. 15¢ 8. $1.10

Page 60
1. C
2. C

This Award Is Presented To

_____

for

★ Doing Your Best

★ Trying Hard

★ Not Giving Up

★ Making a Great Effort